1899

Child of the Divide

Methuen Drama

Published by Methuen 2006

1 3 5 7 9 10 8 6 4 2

First published in 2006 by
Methuen Publishing Limited
11–12 Buckingham Gate
London SW1E 6LB

Methuen Publishing Limited Reg. No. 3543167

A CIP catalogue record for this book is available from
the British Library

ISBN 10: 0 413 77613 1
ISBN 13: 978 0 413 77613 6

Typeset by Country Setting, Kingsdown, Kent
Printed and bound in Great Britain by
Bookmarque Ltd, Croydon, Surrey

Polka Theatre and Tamasha present

Child of the Divide

by Sudha Bhuchar

for Samar, Sinan, Aisha, Sofia and Ayla

Polka and Tamasha gratefully acknowledge the support of

weston kay
Chartered Accountants

Not every firm of chartered accountants is the same

Located in the heart of London's West End

Servicing clients throughout the country

A professional firm dedicated to helping business grow

Let us help you to deal with the current demanding climate of compliance and at the same time, assist you in planning for your own, your family's and your business's future.

To find out more about us and how we can work with you contact Kiran D Patel ACA at:

73/75 Mortimer Street   Tel: 020 7636 7493   Email: k.patel@westonkay.com
London W1W 7SQ   Fax: 020 7636 8424   Website: www.westonkay.com

Partners:
Geoffrey M Davis, Joseph H L Weston, Melvin C Kay, Kiran D Patel, Jill L Springbett

PARTITION

"Partition" means to separate, to divide, to part one from one. For many Indians, this word describes a horror - a moment of madness when families fled their homes to reach safety in a new country. Many died, many more were killed on the way. Around 10 million people moved from one country to another in the summer of 1947, of which as many as 2 million never made it to safety.

The British began ruling India in 1858. By the time of the First World War (1914-1918), when many Indians died in the trenches of France fighting for the British, Indians had begun to dream of independence. These dreams were led by Gandhi and his Congress Party. But the British were not prepared to leave India.

By the time of the Second World War (1939-1945), Gandhi's dreams were joined by the dreams of another man, Jinnah, leader of the Muslim League. Jinnah dreamt that the Muslims of India should have a free country of their own, Pakistan. At the time, Muslims were concentrated mainly in the north and east of the country. He argued that if Britain gave independence and Gandhi's Congress Party won, the Muslims of India would become second-class citizens.

At the end of the War, the British decided to leave India; and, on the terms suggested by Jinnah and the Muslim League. Saddened, Gandhi left the Congress Party and even wanted Jinnah to become India's first Prime Minister, if this would stop the partition of the country.

The British felt that the only way Hindus and Muslims could live together peacefully was to separate the country into two. And so, in 1947, a line was drawn by British officials on the map of India, creating the independent countries of India and Pakistan.

On 14 August 1947, the new country of Pakistan was born.
On 15 August 1947, independent India was born.

Families that had lived together in villages all over north India for countless generations - Hindu families, Muslim families, Sikh families – and had never seen themselves as anything but Indian, woke up one day to find they had to decide whether they belonged to India or to Pakistan. An estimated 10 million people were forced to make this choice, moving their lives across one border to another.

Many Hindu and Sikh families felt they would not be safe in the new country of Pakistan; and many Muslim families felt the same about the new country of India. And so began, in the summer of 1947, the biggest movement of people in history. Men, women and children packed their belongings into as many bags as they could carry and left their ancestral homes to make new lives in new countries. They travelled mainly by foot and by train, in long convoys of hundreds of people, hoping that their numbers would ensure their safety. That was not always the case.

On the way, many convoys were attacked by angry mobs of men drunk on the opportunities for looting, revenge and murder. Mothers and fathers, frightened of losing their children, hid them as best as they could, making them run away to hide in bushes and trees at the first hint of attack. Many lay on top of their children, hoping the mob would kill them and not discover their children. Some took the worst of all choices and killed themselves and their children in any way they could – jumping into rivers and wells, eating poison, setting fire to themselves.

In the middle of this horror, there were also many stories of bravery, of children finding their parents again after being separated, of men intent on killing suddenly changing their minds at the sight of a baby weeping.

On the 30th of January 1948, Gandhi was assassinated by a Hindu fundamentalist in Delhi, after announcing his intention to "walk for peace" to Lahore in Pakistan.

On 11th September 1948, Jinnah died in his sleep, suffering from tuberculosis. His son and grandchildren continue to live in India.

In 1952, Faiz Ahmad Faiz, the greatest of modern Urdu poets, published his poem on Partition - "Freedom Dawn", which concluded:

"This stain-covered daybreak, this night-bitten dawn...
This is not that dawn with longing for which
The friends set out..."

Partition was born out of the dreams of some extraordinary men – men like Gandhi and Jinnah. But it was ordinary Indians – Muslims, Hindus, Sikhs – who had to suffer the nightmare.

Many still suffer, nearly sixty years later.

A map of the newly created states in 1947

Child of the Divide was first performed at Polka Theatre, London, from 5 May - 3 June 2006 with the following cast and creative team:

Cast:

Hasina & Zainab	**Rina Fatania**
Buttameez & Manohar Lal	**Tony Jayawardena**
Pali / Altaaf	**Divian Ladwa**
Aisha & Kaushalya	**Krupa Pattani**
Pagal-Head & Shakur	**Amit Sharma**

Creative Team & Crew:

Director	**Kristine Landon-Smith**
Designer	**Sue Mayes**
Composer	**Arun Ghosh**
Movement Director	**Lawrence Evans**
Lighting Designer	**Ian Scott**
Sound Designer	**Mike Furness**
Production Manager	**Jon Sherwood**
Stage Manager	**Nick Graham**
Deputy Stage Manager	**Nicki Crowther**
Assistant Stage Manager	**Joanne Whitehead**
Wardrobe Manager	**Annie James**
Wardrobe Assistant	**Leni Hill**
Props and Set made by	**Paula Hopkins** **Chloe Cox**
Trainee Director	**Jonathan Man**
Observer	**Mandy Aujla**

Polka and Tamasha would like to thank:
The Entertainer and Smith Brothers, Eastman Army Camp and Party Party

Biographies

Rina Fatania

Rina trained for 3 years at The Central School of Speech and Drama. Her recent credits include Kiran in The Deranged Marriage - Rifco Arts, Pushpa/Hina Shah in Strictly Dandia - Tamasha, Swing cover for Shanti and Mumtaaz in Bombay Dreams - Really Useful Group, Marijana/Dunzazaad in Arabian Nights - Midland Arts Centre, Zara Khan in Dil Ke Baat - Women in Theatre, Euphranor/Bully in Before The City - Vital Stages, and Dame Dolly in Puff the Magic Dragon - Hurricane Productions. Other roles include Billy Downs in The Libertine, Rhonda in The Secret Rapture, Juliette in Mephisto, Jacqueline/Irene in Reader, Rachel in The Sea, Grusha in The Caucasian Chalk Circle, Mistress Overdone/Mariana in Measure for Measure, Moth in Loves Labours Lost and Kaleria in Summerfolk. On radio she has played Meghna in Oceans Unite Us and Boetian/Ensemble in Lysistrata - BBC World Service.

Tony Jayawardena

Tony graduated from the Guildhall School of Music and Drama in 2003. He was awarded a Gold Medal for his theatrical performances at drama school and graduated with Honours. Since leaving drama school Tony has been working consistently in film, television and theatre. His film and television credits include: Chasing Liberty - Warner Brothers, Hotel Babylon – BBC, Doctors – BBC, Holby - BBC. Theatre credits include: Jungle Book as 'Baloo' - Birmingham Stage Company (No.1 Tour), Othello as Montano and The Sneeze - Good Company (Shakespeare) Productions (No.1 Tour). Drama school productions include: Pravda playing Andrew May, Singer playing Pete Singer, The Old Bachelor playing Sir Joseph Wittoll, Trojan Women playing Agammemnon, Landscape playing Duff, The King of Hearts playing Genevieve, A Midsummer Night's Dream playing Demetrius, Snout and Mustardseed, Barbarians playing Redozubov and Robert Zucco. Tony is delighted to be joining the cast of Child of the Divide for Polka Theatre and Tamasha.

Divian Ladwa

Divian's theatre credits include Tamasha's Strictly Dandia (King's Theatre Edinburgh, The Lyric Hammersmith), The Trouble with Asian Men - artsdepot, A Fine Balance - Hampstead Theatre, Fluxx Improvisational Theatre Company's Alls Hallow and Even with Trudie and Jeff and various shows of The Visitor and a London tour of Spare Tyre's Burning. His TV and Film credits include a commercial for London's Fuller Pride, an ident for Indian channel Aaj Tak's sports programme, School's Out - Channel 4, short features by Imagination Films including Modern Chivalry and Painful Love and Wing Kit Loois' 'Tomorrow' – in which he co-choreographed the movies' fight scene. Divian can be seen in the British feature film SAXON (dir. Greg Loftin) playing Rahim and he is finishing work on his own short film 'The Boxer'.

Krupa Pattani

Krupa graduated last October from the University of Winchester with a degree in Performing Arts. She is due to start training at Drama Studio London this summer. Child of the Divide is Krupa's first project with Tamasha Theatre Company and she is extremely delighted to be a member of a very talented cast and team. Her theatre credits include; Tony and Guy: Face of Hampshire – Chosen, Freedon Inneh/Donovan Farquarson, This is For You – A Dangerous Time To Be Defined, Performing Arts Dissertation Performance – University of Winchester, Musical Madness – KASPA, Pizza in Africa – KASPA, All Men Are B*****ds – Bodens, Twilight Zone – KASPA. Film credits include: The Witches Hammer – Amber Pictures, Destination Brixton Da Film – Bosscrown Film Productions. Film credits for Burnhand Film Productions - Tenderness, Give and Take, The Bond. Television roles include: Casualty – BBC Television. Krupa would like to thank her Mum, Dad, family, friends, Tom, Paul, Gregory and JPA Management for their invaluable support and advice.

Amit Sharma

Amit is a graduate of Graeae's The Missing Piece 1 project. This is Amit's second production with Tamasha after appearing in A Fine Balance (Hampstead Theatre). His other theatre credits include: Other People's Shoes - Theatre Royal Stratford East and Spare Tyre, Woyzeck, Into The Mystic, The Trouble With Richard, Diary Of An Action Man - Graeae, Granny and the Gorilla - Unicorn, Reality Check - Theatre Centre, Something Else - Tall Stories, as well as others. He was also Assistant Director on The Changeling – Graeae and The Dysasters of John Daniell - Immediate Theatre. TV and Film credits include: Tikkabilla - BBC, The Robinsons - BBC, Waiting for Movement - Red Leader.

Amit co-wrote 'Stoppage Time' - BBC Radio 4, as well as writing 'Indi-yaar' for Paines Plough's Wild Lunch series. If Amit's not doing any of the above then he plays a supporting role to the current Champions of Europe, Liverpool Football Club!

Sudha Bhuchar (Writer)
Sudha is joint founder and Artistic Director of Tamasha. She is both an actor and a playwright. She played Dina Dalal in Tamasha's A Fine Balance (based on the novel by Rohinton Mistry) at Hampstead Theatre in January 2006. Her many acting credits include, Murder - BBC, EastEnders - BBC, Doctors - BBC, Holby City - BBC and Haroun and the Sea of Stories - Royal National Theatre and she is a regular on the BBC Radio drama Silverstreet. Her writing credits for Tamasha include, Fourteen Songs, Two Weddings and A Funeral, Balti Kings and Strictly Dandia, in which she also performed. She writes regularly with Shaheen Khan and their many credits include 3 series of Girlies for BBC Radio 4 and Balti Kings (stage play as well a six part series for Radio 4). Their screenplay, The House Across the Street, has been shown on BBC 4 as part of a new writers initiative and they have co-written an episode of Doctors for the BBC. Sudha also co-wrote a short film Midnight Feast, which was screened at the 11th Raindance Film Festival. Child of the Divide is her first children's play. Sudha jointly won, with Kristine Landon-Smith, the 2005 Asian Women of Achievement Award for Arts and Culture.

Kristine Landon-Smith (Director)
Kristine is joint founder and Artistic Director of Tamasha and has also directed all of the company's shows. Her 1996 production, East is East, was nominated for an Olivier award and her original production of Fourteen Songs, Two Weddings and A Funeral won the Barclays Theatre Award for Best New Musical. Her most recent show, Strictly Dandia, enjoyed critical acclaim and sell-out success at the Lyric Hammersmith during January and February in both 2004 and 2005. Other freelance directing work has been with The Royal Court Theatre, Bristol Old Vic, Palace Theatre Westcliff, Nitro, Yellow Earth Theatre and has recently worked with the Royal Danish Theatre to direct Con:FUSIONS Workshop in autumn 2005, which was aimed at developing cultural diversity in Scandinavian theatre. She has also recently been producing for the World Service Soap Westway. Kristine has also directed her first short film Midnight Feast, which went on to be screened at the 11th Raindance Film Festival. Her work for BBC Radio has included many productions of which A Yearning and Women of the Dust won CRE Race in the Media Awards. She has directed a production of Lysistrata – an adaptation by Ranjit Bolt – for the BBC World Service. In November 2005 Kristine directed The Trouble with Asian Men at artsdepot and in January 2006 directed A Fine Balance (based on the novel by Rohinton Mistry) at Hampstead Theatre.

Arun Ghosh (Composer)
Manchester-based composer and musician, Arun composes works for the theatre and the media including the soundscape for Storm - Contact Theatre, in association with Peshkar Productions and Chol Theatre Company and Mona - Nitrobeat festival, in colloboration with Sonia Hughes and Darren Pritchard. Arun regularly performs, both locally and nationally, with his own bands and others including Speakeasy, Nashini and samba band - Blocofever. He has performed at venues such as the Lowry, Green Room, Night & Day, Band on The Wall, Zion Centre and performed as part of the London Jazz Festival at the Royal Festival Hall in 2002. Constantly increasing his creative repertoire, Arun has branched out into singing, rapping and producing and in recognition of his burgeoning musicianship, recently received the ATOM Award from the PRS Foundation. Arun's recent solo performance set, Freaky Deaky, was part of the May xtrax/decibel performing arts showcase in Manchester.

Sue Mayes (Designer)
Sue Mayes trained at Central School of Art and Design (Central St. Martins) in the 1970's. Her career started at Ipswich Rep, from where she went on to residences at the Belgrade Theatre in Education - Coventry, Contact Theatre - Manchester and The Everyman Theatre - Liverpool. Her freelance work has included designs for: The Royal Shakespeare Company, Talawa Theatre Company, Bristol Old Vic Theatre, and the Theatre Royal Stratford East. Recent designs include Turn of the Screw - Wolsey Theatre, Ipswich and Kafka's Dick - Derby Playhouse. Sue teaches regularly at drama schools across London including R.A.D.A and Guildhall School of Music and Drama, and she has recently moved into film as production designer on Midnight Feast, a short film for Tamasha, and Two Minutes for the BBC. This is Sue's fifteenth design for Tamasha.

Lawrence Evans (Movement Director)

Lawrence works as a director, movement director and actor. He was nominated for an Olivier Award for his work with Tony Harrison at the National Theatre. He has worked with the poet and playwright on all his site-specific theatre pieces touring to Greece, Austria, Sweden and Bradford. He received a Best Actor Award from the Liverpool Echo and Daily Post Northwest Arts Awards and his co-written play Lives Worth Living is published by Heinemann. His work as an actor includes small, middle and large scale touring nationally and internationally, many of the regional Repertory Theatres throughout the UK as well as the National Theatre, NT studio, Cheek by Jowl, the Young Vic and Northern Broadsides. As a Movement Director he has done over 40 productions. As a Director his work this year includes the current Christmas show for Oxfordshire Touring Theatre Company, Beauty and the Beast by Mike Kenny, Stravinsky's Soldier's Tale with Anthony Marwood touring with the Academy of St. Martin in the Fields, The Country Wife - Drama Centre London, The Plough and the Stars - East 15 and the New York Showcase for the Conference of Drama Schools. In Drama Schools he has directed at Rose Bruford, Italia Conti, East 15, ALRA and Drama Centre. Other directing credits include: Missing and Water Wings by Rosie Fordham - Theatre Centre and Peace of Pocahontas - Polka. Co-directing credits include: Mother Goose and the Wolf - London Bubble and Breaking China and Souls by Roy Williams (re-tour) - Theatre Centre for which he was also Associate Director in 2001/2. This is Lawrence's third show for Tamasha.

Ian Scott (Lighting Designer)

Ian studied theatre design at Mountview Theatre School and specialises in lighting. He has designed the lighting for many theatre productions throughout the UK and Europe. Companies he has worked with include: Paines Plough, 7:84, Sphinx, Nitro, Royal National Theatre, Traverse Theatre, Almeida, Opera Circus, National Youth Theatre, Actors Touring Company, Abbey Theatre, Citizens Theatre, Nottingham Playhouse, Salisbury Playhouse, Greenwich Theatre, David Glass Ensemble, Polka Theatre, LIFT, Theatre Royal Plymouth, Company of Angels, Gecko, Stan Won't Dance, ColesCéim, Blast Theory and Graeae. An Associate Artist of Suspect Culture, Ian designed both set and lighting for One Two..., Timeless, Candide 2000, Lament, Mainstream and 8000M and the lighting for Airport, Local, Casanova and their forthcoming production, The Escapologist. Alongside his theatre credits, Ian's work in other areas has included the lighting design for the ice-rink at Somerset House, the award-winning Unknown Amazon exhibition at the British Museum and the new lighting installation at the London Planetarium. Ian has just won Best Lighting Design in the Irish Times Theatre Awards 2005.

Mike Furness (Sound Designer)

Theatre sound designs include: All's Well That Ends Well and As You Like It - RSC at the Barbican. Blues In The Night, The Witches, Ladyday, The BFG - West End, Mother Courage - National Theatre. He has also designed sound for: Birmingham Rep, Manchester Library, The Kings Head, The Tricycle, Paines Plough, Theatre Royal Stratford East and the Brighton and Edinburgh Festivals. He has produced a series of audio dramas for The Natural History museum and also a number of Talking Books. His production of Music for Fireworks ranges from events such as The Royal Windsor Horse Show to the launch of the P&O Cruise Ship "Oriana" The majority of his work is designing sound systems for concerts, corporate, and other live events worldwide, most recently for Ford, EMI & MTV. This is his eighth sound design for Tamasha.

Polka Theatre

Polka Theatre is one of the few venues in the UK which is dedicated exclusively to producing and presenting high quality theatre for young audiences. Since our doors opened in 1979, this unique venue has offered children a first taste of the thrilling, challenging and inspiring world of theatre.

"Polka is a place of magic and wonder, an inspiration to any child's imagination." The Sunday Times

Polka aims to stimulate young people's passion for theatre by providing them with the widest possible range of experiences: from the thrilling drama of **Child of the Divide** (5 May - 3 June 06); classic tales such as **The Little Mermaid** (7 June - 1 July 06); interactive performances for under 5s like **Martin Waddell's Bear Stories** (29 June - 5 August 06); and experimental theatre, such as 2003's groundbreaking installation performance **Best Behaviour,** described by The Guardian as *"the best piece of theatre this century".*

At Polka, there's space to play, to laugh, to discover, to create... with something for all ages, from toddlers to teenagers. It's a magical place where you can steal a rare moment to share with your children. No two visits are the same...you'll soon see why Polka is where theatre begins!

Polka Theatre 240 The Broadway, Wimbledon London, SW19 1SB

TICKETS 020 8543 4888
www.polkatheatre.com

Tamasha

Tamasha is the London-based company dedicated to creating theatre from a uniquely British Asian sensibility. Our productions are characterised by their cultural richness, universal relevance, and power to show the big picture through the small story. Be it in a Birmingham curry house kitchen or at a summer festival in the Punjab, Tamasha aims to 'create a drama' out of the untold stories of people's lives.

From adaptations of classic literature through improvised comedy and vibrant musicals, to groundbreaking new writing, Tamasha has played a key role in driving the crossover of Asian culture into the British mainstream. Successes like **East is East, Fourteen Songs Two Weddings and a Funeral** and **A Fine Balance** have won acclaim from critics and audiences alike, and have launched the careers of a number of well-known British Asian artists. Since its founding in 1989 by director Kristine Landon-Smith and playwright/actress Sudha Bhuchar, Tamasha has produced 16 new plays, and has won a number of awards, including a Barclays Theatre Award and an Oliver nomination for Best Musical.

Alongside touring productions, Tamasha Developing Artists nurtures the individuality of the theatre artists of tomorrow, while our distinct brand of education work celebrates the rich diversity of Britain's young people and uses theatre to foster cultural confidence in schools.

Child of the Divide is Tamasha's first play for children.

For more about our work, or to join our mailing list, visit www.tamasha.org.uk

tamasha

Tamasha gives thanks to the following companies, trusts, foundations and individuals for their ongoing support::

Café Lazeez; Cobra Beer Ltd; Bank of Ireland; The John S Cohen Foundation; Esmée Fairbairn Foundation; The Stanley Picker Trust; The Puri Foundation; Royal Victoria Hall Foundation; Garfield Weston Foundation; Anuj J Chande; Régis Cochefert; Shernaz Engineer; Zulf Masters, OBE; Nina & Nilesh Majeethia; Deepa Patel; Kiran Patel; James L. Prouty; Mayank & Vandana Shah; Rahul & Rita Sharma; Ramesh & Ella Vala; together with those who wish to remain anonymous.

Glossary of non-English words

A salaam walaikum	'Peace be with you'
Allah ki kasam	'I swear by Allah'
Atma is Amar	'Soul is eternal'
Abu	Father
Al ham dullilah	'Praise be to Allah'
Allah	One true God
Ammi	Mother
Annas	Item of currency
Azan / Azaan	Call to prayer
Bacho	Children
Bada aaya	'Who do you think you are?'
Badmash	Villian (used endearingly if about a child)
Bahen	Sister
Baisakhi	Harvest festival in Punjab
Bakwaas	Nonsense
Bande	People
Bante	Marbles
Baraat	Groom's wedding procession
Beta	Child
Bhai sahib	Respected term for brother
Bhajo	Run
Budda	Old man
Burra aadmi	Big man
Chalo	'Let's go'
Chunri	Long scarf
Daal	Lentils
Dada	Grandfather (on father's side)
Dadi	Grandmother (on father's side)
Darpok	Coward
Darvaza kholo	'Open the door'
Desh	Country
Dhoti	A long cloth worn by Hindu men
Diwali	Hindu festival of lights
Dua (du'a)	Personal prayer to God, 'calling on God'
Dupatta	A type of head covering
Gajar ka halva	A pudding made from carrots and milk
Hai meri	'Oh My!'
Idd	Islamic festival (also spelled id, eid)
Idhar anna	'Come here'
Inshallah (insha allah)	'Allah willing' or 'God willing'
Jaadu ki pudiya	Little packet of magic
Jaldi	Quickly
Kafir	Non believer
Kagaz	Paper
Kalma	Muslim Oath: Literally 'there is only one God and Mohammed is his Prophet'

Kasti	Boat
Kazi	Judge
Keema	Mince meat
Khala	Aunt (mother's sister)
Khatais	A type of biscuit
Kheer	Pudding made from rice and milk
Khuda hafiz	'May God be with you'
Kiddan!	'How's it going?'
Kudhi	Girl
La illaha il lalha, Mohammed rasul Allah	'There is no God but Allah and Mohammed is his prophet'
Laddous	A type of sweet
Lathi	Stick
Lori	Lullaby
Maidan	Open ground
Mama kilti	Pali's baby name for quilt
Manj	clean
Maro isko	Hit him
Masuum	Innocent
Mataji	Mother
Mohalla	Neighbourhood
Mohammed	The "prophet" and founder of Islam
Mosque	Islamic place of worship
Murghi	Chicken
Namaaz	Prayer
Namaste	Hindu greeting
Nana	Grandfather (on mother's side)
Nani	Grandmother (on mother's side)
Paisa	A unit of currency rather like pence
Pariah	Outsider
Pitaji	(Hindu) father
Pithu	A game played with piled up stones
Pupha	Uncle (father's sister's husband)
Rabba	My God
Rakhi	Decorative thread
Rehn de	Leave it
Shami kebabs	Kebabs made from mince meat
Shukar al ham dullillah	Thanks be to Allah
Soja	Go to sleep
Soné	My beautiful
Suna	'I hear'
Taar	Wire
Taré	Stars
Theeka	Alright
Toba	'Dear God'
Tonga wallahs	Horse and cart drivers
Tulsi	Basil plant which is holy to Hindus
Walaikum salaam (wa'laykum Salaam)	'And be with you peace'

Child of the Divide

Characters

Pali (*later* **Altaaf**)
Manohar Lal, *his father*
Kaushalya, *his mother*
First Refugee
Second Refugee
Shakur
Zainab, *his wife*
Maulvi, *Muslim priest*
Official
Aisha
Hasina
Buttameez
Pagal Head
Man
Woman

Act One

Sounds of fireworks and jubilant crowds melt into urgent sound of lorries revving up.

Shouts are heard along the lines of 'Lorries are leaving for the border,' 'Hurry . . . Jaldi,' etc.

Scene One

Pali's *house.*

Lights come up on **Pali**, *a boy of nearly five, with his parents,* **Manohar Lal** *and* **Kaushalya**, *in their house. They have a few possessions in bundles and a suitcase, clearly as though they are leaving.* **Kaushalya** *is carrying a baby in her arms. She is looking around the place, not wanting to go. The offstage sounds continue.*

Manohar Lal   Chalo Kaushalya. We agreed. No looking back.

Pali   I want to take my marbles.

Kaushalya   What will you do with them?

Pali   My marbles from my secret hidey-hole!

Manohar Lal   Your mother had to bury her bridal jewellery. Everything will be safe.

Kaushalya   A married woman with a bare neck and wrists . . .

Manohar Lal   Don't look for omens, Kaushalya. This is real. (*To* **Pali**.) We'll buy you marbles there.

Pali   I don't want to go.

Kaushalya   We have no choice . . .

Pali   But my friends?

Kaushalya   You'll make new friends.

Pali   I want the same friends.

Manohar Lal One day, God willing, we'll come back home.

Pali Where are we going?

Manohar Lal Across the border. India.

Pali This is India.

Manohar Lal It was. But not any more . . .

(*Internal voice.*)
  How to say to my boy
  The soil he stands on
  No longer welcomes him as a son?

(*To* **Pali**.) Now they've made this into a new country. Pakistan.

Pali Did God make it?

Manohar Lal Not God . . .

Pali Who then?

Kaushalya So many questions.

Manohar Lal People . . . the white rulers . . . and us who
don't trust ourselves to live together.

Pali I didn't see you make it.

A huge firework is let off. **Pali** *gets very scared.*

Manohar Lal It's all right, son. Just the freedom celebrations.

Pali Scaring me.

Kaushalya Adults are jumping out of their skins, let alone
children.

Manohar Lal (*internal voice*)
  Fireworks drown
  Screams and cries
  Of people divided.
  A new dawn, they said,
  And carved my country in two.
  Borders and lines
  The price of freedom.

Hindus to the right,
Muslims to the left.
I bundle up my family
And follow blind.
I would have liked a say
In our fate.

(*To* **Kaushalya**.) We're in the hands of God.

Kaushalya   God has lost his faith today. Where does it leave us?

Pali   If I die, will my soul come back?

Kaushalya   Shh . . . You have your whole life ahead of you.

Manohar Lal   Your soul is everlasting, son. Atma is Amar. No sword can kill it or water drown it, nor can fire burn it or wind dry it.

Kaushalya   Don't encourage him.

Pali   When Pitaji's a grandad and you're a grandma, you'll die and me and Gudiya (*Meaning the baby.*) will be on our own.

Kaushalya   You'll have each other. (*Looking at the thread round* **Pali***'s wrist.*) This rakhi she tied on you . . .

Pali   She didn't tie it . . . she's a baby.

Kaushalya   You know what it means?

Pali   I know, I have to look after her for ever . . .

Kaushalya   And her prayers will keep you safe.

Pali   She can't pray.

An urgent voice from outside shouting something along the lines of 'It's not safe for Hindus. Lorries are leaving for the border. Hurry.'

Scene Two

Outside, near where the lorries are leaving.

Manohar Lal   Come on.

He gathers his family and their few possessions together. **Pali** *tries to rush back as he's forgotten something, but* **Manohar Lal** *stops him.*

Pali   My mama-kilti. (*His baby word for quilt.*)

Manohar Lal   Leave it.

Kaushalya   He can't sleep without his quilt.

Manohar Lal *reluctantly runs and gets it as a movement section begins during which the Hindus are scrambling to get on the lorries. There is a great storm of action as people throw luggage on and others get disgruntled as they throw it off to make room for more people. Improvisation of very sparse dialogue. People scramble onto the lorries and others complain of being squashed.* **Kaushalya** *gets on with the baby, but as* **Manohar Lal** *is about to do so he realises that* **Pali** *is no longer holding on to his finger. He starts shouting for him as the lorry revs-up to go.*

First Refugee   Get in, get in.

Manohar Lal   Pali! Pali!

Second Refugee   Get in. He'll get on another lorry.

Kaushalya   Hai! Hai! Stop the lorry. Pali!

First Refugee   Get on or off.

Second Refugee   You want to look for your child? Look. Let us go!

Kaushalya*'s screams get louder as the lorry moves off.*

Scene Three

Shakur *and* **Zainab***'s house.*

Pali *is asleep in* **Zainab***'s lap, wrapped in his quilt. She is holding him quietly.*

Shakur   Why so silent, Zainab?

Zainab   Too scared to speak.

Shakur (*internal voice*)
Even in fear
She looks more beautiful
Than before.
Complete
His little body
Clinging to her curves.
Pariah, yet still
A perfect fit.

(*To* **Zainab**.) All the Hindus have left their homes. They've gone for good.

Zainab   Maybe we should leave him from where you picked him up. I'm scared we'll be cursed.

Shakur   Others are looting shops, stealing wives. They should be cursed. We are giving a child shelter, Zainab. We will be rewarded.

Zainab (*internal voice*)
How I have longed to look
Into the eyes of my son,
Blackened with kajal,
To keep him safe.

(*To* **Shakur**.) My lap has been empty all these years . . .

Shakur   God works in mysterious ways.

Zainab   He's not ours. How can we keep him?

Shakur   The lorries have gone, Zainab. Allah only knows if his parents are alive.

Zainab   Promise me, Shakur, you looked everywhere for them.

Shakur   *Allah ki kasam.* I was selling my china and pande in Nanakpura when I realised all the Hindus had left. There was only this boy at the end of the lane, crying for his pitaji. I took his hand and said, 'Come, we'll find your father!' He took me to the place from where the convoy of lorries had left, but by then even the dust raised by them had long since settled and the place was deserted. It was dark. So I picked him up and brought him home. He was so tired, he fell asleep on my shoulders.

Zainab   Poor thing. Three days he's been crying for his mataji and pitaji.

Shakur   Even if we took him to the police, they can't restore him to his parents.

Zainab   We are God-fearing people. You have done what you can.

She looks at the sleeping **Pali**.

Zainab (*internal voice*)
   I would shut my ears
   To the lullabies
   Of mothers,
   Their sweet voices
   Mocking my pain.
   Dare I hope
   To sing him a lori
   Of my own?

(*To* **Shakur**.) What's his name?

Shakur   When I asked him he said Pali.

Zainab   These Hindus have such odd names. If I'd had a son, I would have called him Altaaf.

Shakur   Well, from today he is Altaaf. We have found a son and he has found parents.

Pali *wakes up and starts to cry again.*

Zainab   Cry, son. Let the ocean out or you'll drown inside.

She comforts him.

He's so little.

Just then **Aisha**, *a little girl of about six, appears at the doorway. She is unkempt with matted hair, but is a complete live wire, older than her years.* **Zainab** *and* **Shakur** *realise she is there.*

Zainab   How many times I've told you not to creep up on people?

Aisha   Ammi's really depressed today so your clothes aren't ready.

Zainab   Your mother! I told her I needed that suit for Idd. Has she fed you today?

Aisha   She forgot.

Pali *recognises* **Aisha**. **Shakur** *and* **Zainab** *get concerned.*

Pali   Aisha!

Zainab   You know him?

Aisha   He's from my mohalla. (*To* **Pali**.) Ammi said you'd gone to India like all the other Hindus.

Pali   I got lost . . . Pitaji and Mataji are gone . . .

Aisha   Wish my ammi would get lost.

Zainab   *Toba toba.* Don't say that.

Aisha   It's true.

Shakur (*to* **Pali**)   You can stay here till your pitaji and mataji come for you.

Aisha   Zainab mani is nice. She feeds me orange rice.

Pali   When will they come?

Shakur   Inshallah soon.

Pali (*sees a cat in the courtyard and gets distracted*)   Look, a cat.

Aisha   Where?

Pali   There. He's jumped off the wall.

Aisha   It's chasing the butterfly. Come on, lets run after it.

Zainab   No! Stay inside.

Pali   Can Aisha stay and play?

Aisha   Please!

Zainab (*internal voice*)
Let me keep him
To myself,
Just until
I know
I can make him mine.

Shakur   Let them play.

Zainab   Just for a while, but don't tell your ammi about Pali.

Aisha   Why?

Zainab   Just promise.

Aisha   *Allah ki kasam.*

Zainab   I'll bring you two some milk and khatais.

She indicates that **Shakur** *should come to one side.*

Zainab   If Aisha knows him, he will be recognised by others.

Shakur   He's only safe within these four walls.

Zainab *leaves.*

Pali   Why am I a secret?

Aisha   Hindus have to hide or run away.

Pali   Like the butterfly.

Aisha   It's flown away to find a friend, but you have a friend.

Pali   You. And I'm your secret.

Aisha   My ammi says secrets are special.

Pali   My mataji said to never have secrets. To tell her everything.

Aisha   My ammi tells me everything but then she makes me cross my heart and hope to die.

Pali   I hope you don't die.

Aisha   I won't, silly. Can you do a butterfly with your hands?

Pali *copies her, with his quilt still wrapped around him.*

Pali   I like butterflies because they've got nice colours and patterns on them.

Aisha   They are like snails but they've got wings.

Pali   Snails carry their houses but butterflies are born from their houses.

Aisha (*touching his quilt*)   You look like a butterfly wrapped with this. Are these your wings?

Pali   It's my mama-kilti. When I was little, I couldn't say 'quilt'. It's from Mataji's old saris.

Zainab (*returning with their snacks*)   Here, bacho. Shami kebabs and fresh khatais.

Pali *grabs a kebab and attacks it hungrily.*

Aisha   You can't eat those. It's meat.

Zainab   It's keema. Eat if you're hungry, beta.

Shakur   Should you have done that?

Zainab   There are worse sins.

Shakur   You will win him through his stomach like you did me.

Zainab   It's nice to see him smiling at last.

There is a loud and ominous knock on the door.

Zainab   They've come. The people to whom he belongs.

Shakur   Could be anyone.

Another blow at the door, like a lathi crashing against it.

Maulvi (*off*)   *Darvaza kholo!* Open the door!

Zainab   Go inside, bacho! Stay quiet.

Pali   I'm scared.

Aisha   I'm not.

Shakur *goes to open the door and* **Zainab** *puts on her veil (she is in purdah in front of men other than her husband). The* **Maulvi** *enters.*

Shakur   *A salaam walaikum*, Maulvi sahib.

Maulvi   *Walaikum salaam.* Suna, he says you are harbouring a non-believer in the house, a kafir boy.

Shakur   I have no kafir.

Maulvi   The townsmen are ready to raid your place, Shakur bhai, so if you have something to confess . . .

Shakur   Maulvi sahib, I have only given shelter to an orphan boy.

Maulvi   Bring him out to me. At once.

Zainab   I have adopted the child, Maulvi sahib. Is it a sin to adopt a child?

Maulvi   In front of whom have you adopted this child? Was there a Kazi? Witness?

Shakur   Allah is our witness.

Maulvi   You don't fear the wrath of Allah, bahen? You give a non-believer a place in your lap?

Zainab   He's just a small boy.

Maulvi   Does he know the Kalma?

Shakur   We'll teach him.

Maulvi   Have you had him circumcised?

Silence. Clearly **Shakur** *and* **Zainab** *hadn't thought of that.*

Maulvi   Bring him to the mosque tomorrow. We'll whisper the azan in his ear, give him a Muslim name and do the circumcision.

Zainab   We'll bring him, Maulvi sahib. We'll make him our son, Altaaf, in front of the whole town.

Maulvi   On judgement day Allah will reward you for this. *Khuda hafiz.*

Shakur *and* **Zainab**   *Khuda hafiz.*

The **Maulvi** *leaves.*

Zainab
Shukar al ham dullillah.
We don't have to hide
Like thieves
With stolen goods.
We can display our treasure
For the world to see.

Scene Four

The mosque, the next day.

Pali *is at the mosque with* **Shakur** *and the* **Maulvi**. *He still has his little quilt around him. The* **Maulvi** *whispers the azan (call to prayer) in his ear and this can be heard by the audience, signifying that* **Pali** *is being invited into the religion. He looks very scared. The* **Maulvi** *then starts to read the Kalma.*

Maulvi   *La illaha il lalha, Mohammed rasul Allah.* Repeat after me. There is only one God and Mohammed is his prophet.

Pali *(holding on to* **Zainab***'s legs)*   Don't want to.

Zainab   Say what Maulvi sahib is asking, son.

Maulvi   Don't you want God's love?

Pali (*upset*)   God is inside everybody. Pitaji said he's in my blood.

Zainab (*internal voice*)
   I too feel
   My Allah
   As real
   As the pulse
   On my wrist.
   Still we are told
   There is them
   And there is us.

Maulvi   Only if you believe will God protect you. Once you are a Muslim, nobody will ask who you were before.

Pali   Don't want to say it!

Shakur (*internal voice*)
   My God
   Protects the good
   And the innocent.
   On my life's actions
   He passes judgement.
   Am I doing right, my Allah,
   By this masuum boy
   You have placed
   In my custody?

Shakur   You're scaring him, Maulvi sahib.

Maulvi   With the mobs still running wild looking for non-believers, he should be scared.

Shakur   I promise you, I will make him say it. Please let's finish the other necessaries.

The **Maulvi** *sees the red rakhi thread that is on* **Pali**'s *wrist, and with a knife forcefully cuts it.* **Pali** *starts crying.*

Pali   Gudiya!

He carries on crying 'Gudiya!' while holding on to **Zainab**.

Maulvi (*putting a red rumi cap onto the boy's head*)   *Al ham dullilah.* Now he is your boy and will have our protection. Congratulations!

Pali (*internal voice*)
  He cut off the thread, Mataji.
  I'm sorry,
  It's not my fault,
  They didn't stop him.
  What will happen
  To Gudiya
  Now the thread is cut
  And I can't protect her?
  I'm sorry, Mataji,
  It's not my fault.

Scene Five

A refugee camp on the Indian side of the border.

We see **Manohar Lal** *and* **Kaushalya** *with their possessions.*
Kaushalya *places the baby on the floor and puts her dupatta over the face of the child, indicating that the baby has died. She beats her chest in grief and calls out.*

Kaushalya
  Hai meri Gudiya
  Jaadu ki pudiya!
  My baby doll,
  Why am I still here
  And you are gone?
  God should have taken me, Manohar Lal.
  A mother should go
  Before her children.
  You should have made him
  Take me.

Manohar Lal   *Bus Kaushalya* . . . Shh now.

Kaushalya   Don't try to console me, who couldn't save her flesh and blood.

Manohar Lal   None of us were safe from the mob that attacked our lorries.

Kaushalya   Yet we are alive, while my Gudiya was crushed like grain between stones.

Manohar Lal
Kiss her goodbye,
Set her soul free.
She was too good
For this world.
Let her come back
In less troubled times.

Kaushalya   Tell me what sins have I committed to see both my children snatched from me?

Manohar Lal   You have done nothing, Kaushalya. It is the world that has gone mad.

Kaushalya   Where is my Pali? My first baby . . . love of my life, the life in my love. I need to know what has happened to my boy. I would shout at him at the smallest thing. Empty anger over spilt daal and dirt. Rabba, restore to me my precious. His strong arms have to be my strength when I am old and grey.

Manohar Lal   I will look for him, I promise. There's an office in Delhi to report lost children. When we reach there, I'll go.

Kaushalya   Where is he? His sister tied a rakhi on him to keep him safe.

Scene Six

Shakur *and* **Zainab***'s house.*

Pali *is in the courtyard, dressed in new clothes that clearly show him to be a Muslim boy. He still has his quilt around him. He is looking very festive, which is incongruous with his mood. He is drawing a picture in the dirt with a stick. It is his mother and father and a baby.* **Zainab** *enters wearing a bright suit and carrying a tray of laddoos. She goes and offers one to* **Pali**. *He shrugs and refuses.*

Zainab   Do you know why we had a party?

Pali *shakes his head.*

Zainab   For you. To welcome you as Altaaf, our son.

Pali   My name is Pali.

Zainab   It's not safe for you to be Pali anymore. Do you understand that, son?

Pali *shakes his head, clearly not understanding. Silence as* **Zainab** *notices the drawing* **Pali** *has made.*

Zainab   Is this your pitaji and mataji?

Pali *nods.*

Zainab   And the baby?

Pali   Gudiya. Mataji grew her in her tummy. Then she came out and cried so much, I couldn't sleep.

Zainab   I know I didn't grow you from my flesh, but I want more than anything in the world to give you a mother's love.

Pali   You're not my mum.

Zainab   You know I prayed and prayed and asked dua from Allah to make me a mother. Twice he answered my prayers and both times it was not to be. Then he sent you to me.

Pali (*wrapping his quilt around him and starting to cry*)   I want my mataji!

Zainab   Cry, son . . . let the ocean out.

Pali   It's a river.

Zainab   And one day it will only be a puddle. Shall we make a paper boat and float the sadness away ?

Pali   My soul hurts.

Zainab *holds him tight. He lets her. She starts to sing a lullaby.*

Zainab (*singing*)
    Sleep my little prince,
    Soja,
    Sail away
    On a kasti of dreams
    Beyond the moon
    To a magic land
    Of fairies and kings
    Where your princess awaits
    With a garland of love;
    Sleep my little prince,
    Soja.

Scene Seven

Office in Delhi.

Manohar Lal *and* **Kaushalya** *are filing the case for* **Pali** *being missing*

Official (*as he is writing on the form*)   Yashpal , aged five, known as Pali. Why do people give their sons stupid nicknames like Pali? Palis, Rajus and Guddus are two a paisa. Makes our job harder than looking for a speck of dirt in a sack of chapati flour. My father had the good sense to nickname me Bhundal . . . I hated it as a child . . .

Manohar Lal *and* **Kaushalya** *are bemused by his ramblings.*

Official   From *bhondu*, meaning 'simpleton'. Or a harsh translation maybe 'without anything (*Tapping his head.*) up here'.

I used to get teased by bullies, but I'm having the last laugh.
Here I am, an official in this new Indian government serving
the very first Prime Minister, Jawaharlal Nehru, and where are
they? Not bad for a simpleton. So, for example, if I was to get
abducted or lost, you can be sure you will be looking for only
one Bhundal who fits the bill. So where were we? Pali . . . son
of . . . ?

Manohar Lal   Manohar Lal and Kaushalya Rani.

Official   Naranag Mandi, Shikhupura district. Any
distinguishing features?

Kaushalya (*internal voice*)
   His grandfather's eyes,
   An angel's smile,
   Tousled hair
   No comb could tame.
   His eyes twinkle
   And cheeks dimple
   When he smiles
   His monkey smile.

Official   Speak up, I'm a busy man. What shall I fill here?

Manohar Lal   Bhai sahib, he is an ordinary boy. Only to us
he is special. I have a photograph.

Official   Give me, and I will file the case.

Manohar Lal   When will you start looking for him?

Official   When the borders reopen enquiries can begin, but
I don't hold out hope.

Manohar Lal   I can't tell my wife there is no hope.

Official   Bhai sahib, you are young. Don't waste your time
here. Go home and make more babies.

He sees **Manohar Lal**'s *reaction.*

Official   Or embrace another's child. The refugee camps are
full of unclaimed children – lost and littered, like fallen leaves.

Manohar Lal   I have a boy.

Official   He is gone. Accept it.

Manohar Lal   I will never accept it.

There is a physical vignette here, where **Manohar Lal** *is searching and doors are shutting in his face. Sparse dialogue, and possible repetition of the following, ending in his utter despair and internal cry.*

Manohar Lal   Have you seen my Pali?

Voice (*off*)   He's gone. Accept it.

Manohar Lal   We lost him before the troubles.

Voice (*off*)   Start a new life. Don't look back.

Manohar Lal   Has he been spotted?

Voice (*off*)   Thousands like him, washed away by the waves of hatred.

Manohar Lal   Has he been seen?

Voice (*off*)   Who looks at another? Everyone is lost in their own turmoil. Go home. Accept it.

Manohar Lal   I can't. I won't.

(*Internal voice.*)
     If he was dead
     Only then
     Can I accept,
     Shed silent tears
     Like for my baby girl.
     But he is across the border,
     I know he is,
     A few miles between,
     The same stars
     Shine on him.

Scene Eight

Across the border in Pakistan. Wasteland outside the refugee camp.

Three years have passed since **Pali** *disappeared.* **Aisha** *and* **Hasina** *come running on. They sing as they hold hands, lean back and swing round and round.* **Aisha** *has subverted the words of a rhyme.* **Pali** *enters. The girls grab him and force him to be twirled round as well.*

Song
    Kikli kaleer di,
    The turban of my brother,
    Dupatta of my bhabi,
    But she loves another.

    She sparkles and she sways,
    She whispers and she sighs.
    Her love is her life
    But she has her ties.

    My brother will come
    Bringing garlands and flowers,
    We'll dance and we'll sing
    But my bhabi's heart cowers.

Hasina *breaks off and falls to the ground, slightly dizzy.*

Hasina   You've changed the words, Aish.

Aisha   My mum taught me. She had a secret love.

Pali   How do you know?

Aisha   Just do . . . She kisses old letters and covers me in sadness.

Hasina   My ammi had to run away from home to marry my abu.

Pali   Why?

Aisha   Was that in India where you lived?

Hasina   Yeah.

She realises she's said too much.

Aisha   My ammi says marriage is a curse, but I love weddings. Dancin' in the baraat . . .

Hasina   The groom on a white horse, his face a mystery behind garlands of jasmine . . .

Pali   'Cos he's ugly as sin.

Aisha   Oy!

Pali   Marriage is for girls.

Aisha   Yeah, but they like marry boys?

Pali   I'm never getting married.

Aisha   I am. To a man with a scooter and a moustache, which tickles when he kisses my belly-button.

Hasina   Aisha!

Pali   Yuck!

Hasina   Have you ever kissed a girl?

Pali   No way.

Buttameez and **Pagal Head**, *two older Muslim boys, run on rolling a bicycle wheel with a stick.* **Pagal Head** *is clearly tougher, a leader-of-the-pack type.* **Pali** *and the girls clearly recognise* **Buttameez**.

Buttameez   *Theeka* Altaaf!

Pali   All right, Buttameez!

Pagal Head   You kudhi, man? Playing with the girls?

Pali   They're my friends.

Pagal Head   What's that you got around you? (*Pulling* **Pali**'*s quilt.*) Dupatta. Hey, smell this, Buttameez.

Buttameez   I know. It's minging, but he won't wash it.

Pagal Head   Why don't you paint your lips red?

Buttameez   Rehn de Pagal Head.

Pali   What kind of name is that?

He makes a circle with his finger on the side of his head to indicate that **Pagal Head** *is mad.*

Pali   Pagal Head!

Pagal Head *gives him an evil look.*

Pali   Just scratching!

Pagal Head   It's 'cos I go mad if anyone mess with my head.

Hasina   We're not scared of you.

Pagal Head   I know you, Cinderella shoes.

Hasina   Hasina.

Pagal Head (*looking at* **Hasina**'s *faded embroidered shoes*)   You that refugee, kudhi, that manj the pande and sweep the houses?

Hasina   I'm not refugee.

Pagal Head   How comes you live on the camp for Indian refugees? You gotta mum and dad?

Hasina   None of your business.

Buttameez   What's wrong with the camp, eh, dude?

Pagal Head   You tell me. You ran away.

Buttameez   That's 'cos they tried to get me adopted.

Hasina   Me too. Except people only want boys, so I'm safe.

Buttameez   Don't want a new family.

Hasina   My ammi will come and get me from India.

Pagal Head   You Muslim girl. You live in Pakistan now. You can't go back to India.

Buttameez   Wanna play bante?

Pali   Yeah, all right.

Aisha   I'll challenge you.

Pagal Head   I only play for high stakes. Winner takes all.

Aisha   You're on.

Buttameez   Teams?

Pagal Head   You and me take on . . . ?

Pali   Altaaf.

Pagal Head   Altaaf and the kudhis against Pagal Head and Buttameez.

Pali   You're on.

Buttameez   I'm like the unbeatable champion . . .

Aisha   Champion from where? India. Well, this is Pakistan, and we'll see who's champion.

Pali   Five marbles each team.

He makes a circle and each team puts five marbles into it. **Pagal Head** *inspects the marbles.*

Pagal Head   New ones. Don't want no tutte phutte. The girls' team can go first.

Aisha *crouches down and, bending her finger back, aims at the circle. She knocks a marble out of the circle and jubilantly swipes all the marbles.*

Aisha   Victory screech!

Her team screech together.

Buttameez   Beginner's luck.

Pagal Head   Double or quits!

Aisha *puts all her marbles into the circle and the other team adds ten marbles to the pile.*

Aisha   Winner goes first.

Pagal Head   Different player, though.

Hasina *aims and misses.* **Buttameez** *aims and hits two marbles.*

Pali   Foul! He touched two bante!

Pagal Head   Kithe foul? It's not foul.

Aisha   Put them back.

Pagal Head   You gonna make me?

Buttameez   Put them back, Pagal Head. I have my go again.

Pagal Head   No. I'm referee, and I say we win.

Pali   You can't be referee. You didn't see.

Pagal Head   He's calling me a liar.

Buttameez   *Rehn de.*

Aisha   You're just a bully.

Pagal Head (*sweeping aside the marbles*)   We win. In your face! You're a disgrace! (*To* **Buttameez**.) Chal. Let's go.

Buttameez *and* **Pagal Head** *leave.*

Hasina   Let's follow them. I know where he hides his stash.

Pali   How d'ya know?

Hasina   I sweep his house. He has a hidey-hole in the back.

Aisha   Come on. Let's get what's ours.

They follow **Pagal Head** *to his house.* **Pali** *has a huge déjà vu moment. He is standing outside his old house. The girls don't notice at first, but having known* **Pali** *from before,* **Aisha** *realises what has happened.*

Hasina   Behind the house. He's dug a hole

Pali   This is my house! That's my hidey-hole.

Hasina   How can it be your house?

Pali   Why didn't you tell me, Aish? Why didn't you tell me that someone took it?

Aisha   I'm the queen of secrets. Didn't want you to get upset.

Hasina   Upset about what?

Aisha   He used to live here.

Pali   Pitaji said it was as old as history.

Aisha   Pagal Head has seen us!

Pagal Head *and* **Buttameez** *come out.*

Pagal Head   What do you want?

Pali   This is my house. My grandad and great-grandad built it.

Aisha   Don't, Altaaf.

Pagal Head   Says who?

Pali   Here my mataji prayed to the tulsi every day. Why is it burnt?

Pagal Head   Who prays to a stupid tree?

Pali   And here I carved my name on the door – P-A-L-E-E.

Aisha   Oh no!

Pagal Head   Thought your name was Altaaf?

Aisha   Let's go.

Pagal Head   You a Hindu darpok! Why you didn't bhajo all the way to India like the others?

Pali   I'm not scared of you . . . mad head!

Pagal Head   My dad's a burra aadmi. He can make people like you disappear. Kaput! And when you die, you can come back as a fish or something. I can put masala on you and fry you on the tava and eat you.

Pali   You can't just take my house.

Pagal Head   In my food chain, there's like me at the top, no maybe my ammi and abu, then me, then my dadi, dada, nani, nanas, puphas, khalas and cousins, then Muslims from India like Buttameez and you, kudhi, (*Meaning* **Hasina**.) then all the animals and birds and right at the bottom is Hindus like you.

Bada aaya . . . call yourself Altaaf? *Pali ka chacha*, this is my dad's house now. Pakistan Zindabad!

Pali *goes to hit* **Pagal Head** *and a fight ensues.*

Aisha *and* **Hasina**   Stop it! (*Etc.*)

Pagal Head   Oy, Buttameez. *Maro isko.*

Buttameez *joins in enthusiastically, displaying an uncharacteristic venom as the girls try to stop the fight.*

Scene Nine

A little while later. **Pali** *is with* **Aisha** *and* **Hasina***.*

Pali *comforts himself with his quilt.* **Hasina** *wipes his bruises.*

Hasina   I didn't know you was Hindu.

Aisha   He's not. Maulvi sahib made him Muslim.

Pali   Pitaji said people are people, but he lied.

Hasina   Some people are just bad.

Aisha   Like that Pagal Head.

Hasina   And Buttameez. I thought he was our friend.

Aisha   We'll get them.

Pali   They're bigger than us.

Aisha   We'll tell Maulvi sahib and your ammi and abu.

Pali   They're not my mum and dad. My real mum and dad lost me.

Hasina   Maybe they're looking for you.

Pali   I wish I was a baby, then they could have carried me like they did Gudiya.

Hasina   Why don't you think about them? If you think about someone really really hard, then they think about you at the same time.

Aisha   That's stupid.

Hasina   It's true. My ammi said.

Pali   I'm scared I'll forget my mataji. (*Burying his head in his quilt.*) But I remember her smell.

Hasina   I think about my ammi all the time, and I know she thinks about me.

Aisha   So why doesn't she come and get you?

Hasina   She thinks I'm safe with my uncle.

Pali   So why are you in the refugee camp?

Hasina   Can I tell you a secret?

Aisha   Not another secret? My heart's gonna burst.

Pali   *Allah ki kasam*, we won't tell.

Hasina   I'm half-half so I got two names. Hasina 'cos my abu said I was his beautiful princess, and Sita which was my secret with my mama.

Pali   Sita? Hindu name like Pali?

Aisha   Lord Ram's wife. We studied it at school. Before all the Hindus left. Now we're not supposed to know. She was kidnapped by that Raavan, isn't it?

Hasina   Sita stayed pure, but like no one believed her and in the end she asked Mother Earth to take her back.

Pali   I thought Ram and Sita had a happy ending.

Hasina   Mama said Sita was too good for this world. But I'm bad. My uncle said that my abu died because of me.

Pali   'S not true.

Hasina   Hindus killed him 'cos he married a Hindu and they don't like that. Bloods shouldn't mix. But mine is.

Pali   If you cut, do you bleed different colours?

Aisha   Don't be stupid.

Hasina   Because of my Muslim blood, my mama sent me
with my uncle to be safe here in Pakistan. Because of my
Hindu blood, my uncle left me by the side of the road. Sitting
on a stone . . . alone. He said he couldn't love me because in
my face he could see the Hindus that killed his brother. I didn't
want my abba to die . . . *Allah ki kasam* . . . I loved him. He
made me and my mama pretty things and – (*Looking at her
battered shoes.*) – decorated my shoes with taré and sequins.
A soft lady found me. She took my hand and brought me to
the camp across the border. I came with other lost children
like Buttameez.

Pali   I never knew that.

Hasina   You're lucky your new mum loves you. She's always
calling you in to eat a sweet rusk or khatai.

Pali   It's like she don't want me to be hungry. But sometimes
her treats stick in my throat and I'm still hungry. I think about
my real mum and dad. Why did they lose me?

Aisha   Wish I could take my ammi to the mum swap-shop.

Hasina   You don't mean it.

Aisha   I do. I always have to hug and kiss her to cheer her
up. It frightens me. When she's angry, I'm calm; when she's
upset, I'm cheerful; when she's silly, I'm silly. She plays tickle-
monster and we laugh and laugh till we cry. Then she can't
stop. She even cries on my birthday and Idd. When she's sad,
I hate her.

Hasina   My amma will come and get me.

Pali   How do you know?

Hasina   I post her a letter every day.

Buttameez *approaches the trio tentatively.*

Pali   Thought you was my friend.

Buttameez   You didn't tell me you was Hindu.

Aisha   And you didn't tell us you was evil.

Buttameez   Don't you know Hindus hate us?

Hasina   Who says?

Buttameez (*to* **Pali**, *not really hearing* **Hasina**)   I wanna know why you hate us.

Pali   I hate you 'cos you hit me.

Buttameez   I hit you 'cos you hate me.

Pali   I don't.

Buttameez   You do. You Hindus told us to leave India.

Pali   And you Muslims told us to leave Pakistan.

Buttameez   I didn't. I wasn't even here.

Pali   And I didn't. I wasn't even there.

Buttameez   I didn't want to leave.

Pali   Nor did I, but I wish I had now.

Buttameez   I just wanted to play bante with my friends.

Pali   Me too.

Buttameez
   But they looked at me
   And turned away
   Their eyes
   Pure enemy.

Pali   I didn't turn away from you. You hit me.

Aisha   Just 'cos that Pagal Head told you to.

Hasina   You should think for yourself, not just follow bullies.

Buttameez (*meaning* **Pali**)   He made me mental. Never seen a Hindu since we walked all the way here to get away from them.

Hasina   Yes you have.

Buttameez   Haven't.

Hasina   You've seen me.

Buttameez   You're not one of them.

Hasina   Half of me is them.

Buttameez   Why didn't you say?

Hasina   Didn't want your hate like my uncle's.

Buttameez   Why should I hate you?

Hasina   You'd look at my face and see the Hindus that killed your family.

Buttameez   You my best friend. Only one from my desh.

Hasina   And Pali . . . Altaaf is my friend.

It sinks in to **Buttameez**.

Buttameez (*to* **Pali**)   Sorry, dude.

Pali   Yeah. Me too.

Aisha   What happened to your family?

Buttameez   Nothing.

Pali   If you don't tell, you might forget.

Buttameez   I want to forget, but it won't let me.

Aisha   Tell us then.

Buttameez   No!

Hasina   Leave him.

Pali   Come on, let's play lame-tag. Bhago, I'm it.

He hops on one leg and chases the others exhuberantly.

Scene Ten

A few months later. India.

Kaushalya *is cleaning as* **Manohar Lal** *bursts in with huge brown packets.*

Manohar Lal   Kaushalya, I'm home.

Kaushalya *barely looks at him and carries on.*

Kaushalya   You're in the way. I'm trying to clean.

Manohar Lal   Leave it. Come, let's go to the Maidan and fly kites.

Kaushalya   The hinge on the door is rusty.

Manohar Lal   I'll fix it later.

Kaushalya   And the walls haven't been whitewashed for two years.

Manohar Lal (*internal voice*)
   She hears
   But won't listen.
   She cleans, she cooks,
   And never sits.
   She looks, but her eyes never meet mine.
   Her ruby red lips, grey and pale,
   Never break into a smile.
   The hands that held mine
   Out of reach,
   Her body turned away,
   Out of touch.

(*To* **Kaushalya**.) Did you hear me, Kaushalya?

He takes huge kites out of the bag

Kaushalya   Why are you back early? You should be at work.

Manohar Lal   Come on. I challenge you to break my taar.

Kaushalya   Are you out of your mind?

Manohar Lal   Please. Don't say no, Kaushalya. Not today.

Kaushalya   You want the whole world to gloat at my sorrow?

Manohar Lal   You want to stay in these four walls for ever?

Kaushalya   I need to finish what I'm doing.

Manohar Lal   You do when nothing needs doing.

Kaushalya   And what would you like me to do? Play like a child when I don't have my child?

Manohar Lal   Do you know what day it is?

Kaushalya   He will be ten. Lost to us for over half his life.

Manohar Lal *sits down, deflated.*

Manohar Lal   If we saw him in the street, would we even recognise him?

Kaushalya   Are you asking me to forget?

Manohar Lal   We could have another child.

Kaushalya   Never.

Manohar Lal   If you would only let me comfort you.

Kaushalya   How can you know my pain?

Manohar Lal   I miss him too, you know.

Kaushalya   How could you let his fingers slip through your hand?

Manohar Lal   Not a day goes past when I don't ask myself that.

Kaushalya   You carried a suitcase, when you should have carried our boy. The suitcase is safe but where is my boy?

(Internal voice.)
　　Too late.
　　I can't swallow them back,
　　The words

I kept
Under lock and key,
Poisoning me inside,
They've escaped
From my lips.
Is it really him I blame
Or is it me
For holding on,
Not daring to let go,
Lest one day
I should forget
My baby ever was
On this earth?

Manohar Lal (*internal voice*)
I ask myself
Again and again,
How could I let go
Of the little hand
That held mine
So tightly?
I felt his grip
Long after
His fingers had slipped.
In the blink of an eye
He disappeared
From sight.
Rabba, take me back
To the place where he was lost,
To the end of the lane
Where in my dream
He still awaits me.

Act Two

Scene One

Two years later. Streets around the town in Pakistan.

Pali *is out peddling china, etc., with* **Shakur**. *They both have a basket over their heads as they cry out. They could use the audience to sell to.*

Pali   Pande! China!

Shakur   English china! *Desi bartan!*

Pali   Tea set, dinner set! Cups and saucers!

Shakur   Lovely designs. Buy them for your daughters!

Pali   Their mother-in-laws will be impressed!

Shakur   And forget to chide them about their sense of dress!

Pali   They can serve tea like English mem-sahibs.

Shakur   Are you a mif?

Pali *(in explanation)*   Milk in first! . . . One lump or two?

Shakur *(showing one of the cups)*   Moonlight rose, all in blue!

Pali *(showing another pattern)*   Lavender rose, for a love that remains true!

Shakur *(very impressed with* **Pali**'s *improvisation)*   Look at you! Not a hair on your chin and you're peddling romance to my punters.

Pali   People want to be promised more than a cup of tea, Abu.

Shakur   Listen to you . . . you imp! The way you shifted those soup bowls to old Mrs Khan! What did you promise her? A kiss?

Pali   No! I said to her, 'So what if you don't serve soup like the English? Use them for kheer or gajar ka halva. The silver paper on the sweets will shine like the silver pattern on the bowls.'

Shakur   With me, her handkerchief remains tightly knotted in her bosom. Yet for you she eagerly untied it and parted with a healthy sum.

Pali   Can we put it towards our shop fund?

Shakur   Yes, 'Shakur Ahmed and Son', or at the rate you're going it should say, 'Altaaf Ahmed and Father'.

Pali   No, Abu. You came before me.

Shakur   What a respectful boy. You've grown up so fast. Your ammi will soon be looking for a bride for you.

Pali   I'll find my own.

Shakur   Acha? Forward in love too?

Pali   Can I ask you something, Abu?

Shakur   Of course.

Pali   How do you know when you love someone?

Shakur   You mean like a girl?

Pali   Like Ammi?

Shakur (*internal voice*)
  In a sea of faces
  She glowed
  Just for me,
  Her deep blue chunri
  Glittering like stars,
  The sun
  In my courtyard.

(*To* **Pali**.) Your ammi crept into my life and then she took over my heart.

Pali   How do you know it's love?

Shakur   You know because your heart races, you feel the breeze with every pore of your skin and you're more alive than you ever will be.

Pali   How do we know we're alive? How do you know we exist?

Shakur   Badmash! I'm a salesman, not philosopher. (*Pinching him.*) I pinch you . . .

Pali   Ouch!

Shakur   You're alive.

They start to walk off and come across **Manohar Lal.**

Manohar Lal   Excuse me, janab. Could you direct me to Naranag Mandi?

Pali *stares at* **Manohar Lal.** *Seeing someone in Hindu attire is unusual.*

Shakur   Han –

Before **Shakur** *can speak,* **Pali** *dives in.*

Pali   You just carry on straight and then left at Zaman Tailors.

Manohar Lal   What used to be Satish Tailors?

Shakur   Yes. You are from around here?

Manohar Lal   Before partition. I lived here.

Shakur   Then you are a son of this soil. Welcome!

Manohar Lal   Thank you.

He goes off. **Shakur** *is concerned.*

Pali   Is he from India?

Shakur   Many Hindus are coming. To see their old homes, maybe.

(*Internal voice.*)
  The borders reopen,
  Neighbours return
  To pick up the threads
  Of a life

Left behind.
What will I say
If he asks again,
Questions
Long answered
Of blood and belonging?

Pali (*assuages* **Shakur**'s *fears as he starts singing nonchalantly*)
Get up, you pious Muslims,
Come for namaaz.
Judgment day is nigh
When the earth will be no more,
Mountains will turn to dust,
Questions will need answers
About your words and deeds,
Take heed. Take heed.
Oh Muslims awaken,
Come for your namaaz!

Shakur   Come on, now. Your ammi will be waiting.

Scene Two

A little while later.

Pali *and* **Hasina** *are sitting on the branch of a tree sucking mangoes, the juice running all over their faces.*

Pali (*looking at* **Hasina**)   Your face is orange and sticky.

Hasina   So is yours.

Pali *wipes his face with the side of his fading quilt.*

Hasina   You still carry that?

Pali   You still have your Cinderella shoes?

Hasina   Don't fit me any more.

Pali   Some boys gotta cummerbund, I got this.

Silence.

Pali   Can you feel the breeze with every pore of your skin?

Hasina   It's windy.

Pali   Yeah, but is your heart thumpin'? Do you feel really alive?

Hasina   Is it a trick question?

Pali   No, just asking.

Hasina   I like you, if that's what you're asking.

Pali (*embarrassed*)   No.

Hasina   I got something to tell you.

Pali   What?

Hasina   The soft lady is getting me adopted.

Pali   Buttameez hasn't got adopted.

Hasina   Yeah, but he lives wild. Girls can't do that.

Pali   Where you going?

Hasina   This old budda came and chose me.

Pali   How old is he?

Hasina   I don't know . . . forty-five, maybe. He's got sweaty hands and he talks in poetry.

Pali   What did he say?

Hasina   His wife died so he wants me to look after him and his children.

Pali   Like a servant?

Hasina   Like a daughter, he said.

Pali   Say no.

Hasina   I can't. The soft lady said all the other refugee children have got homes now, so I can't be fussy.

Pali   What about your mum in India?

Hasina   I send her letters every day, but maybe she's not coming.

Pali   I won't let you go. I'll talk to Ammi and Abu.

Scene Three

A little while later. **Pali**'s *house. Pakistan.*

Pali   Why can't Hasina come and live with us?

Shakur   She's not our responsibility.

Pali   But she's my friend.

Shakur   I can't take in your strays and waifs.

Pali   Just her.

Zainab   You are enough for us, beta.

Pali   But you're not enough for me!

Shakur   Altaaf!

Pali   You don't care that she's gonna be a servant to a budda baba.

Shakur   I'm sure that he will look after her.

Pali   You don't know. You don't know anything about him.

Zainab   You will not speak to your abu like that.

Pali   You don't care what happens to my special friend.

Shakur   You can still see her.

Pali   She won't be able to come out and play.

Zainab   Girls at a certain age can't come out and play anyway. You have to play with boys now.

Pali   Then I'll marry her.

Shakur   What's got into him?

Zainab   You're too young to know what you want.

Pali   You can't read my mind.

Shakur   Watch your tongue. Hanging around with those vagabonds and lafangas, you're getting led astray.

Pali   I love Hasina.

Zainab   It's a crush. You could never marry someone like her.

Pali   Why not?

Zainab   She's refugee. Without family. Without roots.

Pali   You don't know anything about her.

Shakur   And you're the expert.

Zainab   You can't judge the fruit if you don't know what tree it came from.

Pali   I do know. She's from Delhi, India. Her father was Zafar, a tailor. He made clothes and Cinderella shoes for her and combed her hair into pigtails. Her mother was Kamla, a teacher's daughter . . .

Shakur   A Hindu . . .

Pali   So was I a Hindu. You didn't care which tree I came from.

Zainab   You're our boy now. That's all that matters.

Pali   And Hasina's my friend. That's all that matters.

Shakur   We want the best for you.

Pali   But you don't want me to be happy.

Shakur   Trust us to choose what's best for you.

Pali   You said Allah mian says to extend a hand of friendship to everyone, but you hate my friends.

Zainab   Friends are not family.

Pali (*running off*)   You are not my family.

Zainab   Beta!

Shakur   Leave him.

Scene Four

A little while later. In the Maidan.

Buttameez *and* **Aisha** *run on and alternately pile up five stones, as if in the middle of a game of pithu. When the pile is made they both shout out:*

Buttameez *and* **Aisha**   Pithu!

Pali *and* **Hasina** *come on.* **Pali** *is throwing a ball at* **Aisha***, but she finishes the pile before he can catch her.*

Aisha   Our turn again.

Buttameez   I'll break.

Pali *throws the ball to* **Buttameez***, who hits the stones and breaks them.* **Aisha** *runs to get the ball and aims at* **Hasina** *to try and get her legs. She misses, and* **Pagal Head** *comes on and catches the ball. They all stop in their tracks.*

Hasina   You can't play with us.

Pagal Head (*to* **Hasina**)   *Kiddan!* Cucumba cool, kudhi.

Pali   Leave her alone.

Pagal Head   You wanna teach your munda some manners.

Pali   Like your manners, you mean?

Pagal Head (*to* **Hasina**)   You better be friendly, kudhi, 'cos your boyfriend going back to his desh, innit? Then you gonna have to be nice to me . . .

Aisha   You talking bakwaas.

Pagal Head   *Allah ki kasam.* I come to give you de news. But if you don't wanna know.

Buttameez   You got something to say, spill it out.

Pagal Head   Some weirdo babu coming to get you, man. Got a serious style issue. Wearing them dhoti that fly in the wind showing everytin' . . .

Pali   How do you know?

Pagal Head   Came to our house, innit. My abu ready to kill him if he wants the house back, but he just askin' after you.

Pali   I don't believe you.

Pagal Head   Better believe it. He's got the kagaz, papers proving he's your dad. Take you back to Junglistan with him.

Pali   How does he know where I am?

Pagal Head *flashes a smile.* **Pali** *understands that he has told him.*

Buttameez   You told him?

Pagal Head   Just bein' a good citizen.

Buttameez   You shouldn't've done that.

With a stick, **Pagal Head** *manages to whip off* **Pali**'s *quilt.*

Pagal Head   You won't need your minging dupatta.

Pali   Give it back.

Pagal Head   Smell it! His bib. His ma's perfume. Stinks of tutti.

Pali   I'll smash your head in.

Pagal Head   Try it.

He runs off with the quilt. The others follow him and try to stop him.

Needs a wash. I gonna throw it in the river.

Pali   Leave it.

It is too late. **Pagal Head** *has thrown the quilt in the river.* **Buttameez** *grabs him by the collar.*

Buttameez   You gonna fetch that back or I kill you.

Pagal Head   You're jokin'?

Buttameez   Try me.

Pagal Head   What are you? Hindu lover? You wanna be my banda . . . I look after you.

Buttameez   I'm my own banda.

Pagal Head   You on your own, den.

Buttameez   Get it out.

He pushes him by the river and **Pagal Head** *falls in.*

Pagal Head   I can't swim! Help me!

Aisha   Let him drown.

Hasina   We can't do that. Help him.

Pali *rushes in and helps him. They get him out.* **Pagal Head** *is clearly traumatised.*

Aisha   Coward! Calling others darpok.

Pagal Head *is crying, holding on to* **Pali**.

Pali   You're alive. What you cryin' for?

Pagal Head   I thought I was gonna die like all the others.

Buttameez   What others?

Pagal Head   I saw them, the bodies floatin' in the water . . . the river red with blood . . .

Buttameez   There's no bodies.

Pagal Head   The river is full of bodies. Some running as if they could run on water and escape . . .

Pali   What are you talking about?

Pagal Head   The men and my abu chasin', the Hindus . . . the shoutin' and screamin' . . . the men just killing dem and throwin' the bodies in the water . . . I never kill anyone, I promise . . . I never touched no one . . .

Hasina   It's okay.

Pagal Head   I see the black eyes of a boy looking at me. I wasn't gonna do nothing . . . *Allah ki kasam.* But he too scared and jump in the water hisself. He can't swim. I see him sinking . . . just like a stone . . . sinking to the bottom of the water.

The kids comfort **Pagal Head** *by their presence, not necessarily being able to reach out to him fully.*

Scene Five

Pakistan, **Pali***'s house.*

There is a loud knock at the door. **Zainab** *in her purdah comes on.*

Zainab   Who is it?

Manohar Lal (*off*)   My name is Manohar Lal. I am from Hindustan. I need to speak to Mr Shakur Ahmed.

Zainab   Shakur, Shakur, a man has come from Hindustan.

Shakur   Stay inside with Altaaf. Let me talk to him.

He lets **Manohar Lal** *in.*

Manohar Lal   *A salaam walaikum*, Shakur sahib.

Shakur   *Namaste.*

Manohar Lal   We met in the street with the boy . . .

Shakur   My son. Altaaf.

Manohar Lal   He gave me directions. I didn't know . . .

Shakur   Please sit.

Manohar Lal *sits down awkwardly. A clock ticks slowly during this scene.*

Shakur   You have come from far?

Manohar Lal   Delhi.

Shakur   All the way from there? Staying long?

Manohar Lal   As long as it takes.

Shakur   What is your purpose here?

Manohar Lal   I have come for my boy. We lost him when we left this place.

Zainab (*internal voice*)
  This is it,
  The long-dreaded
  Knock at the door,
  But I won't
  Let him go.

Shakur   Hundreds of children got lost in that time.

Manohar Lal   But it is my boy that you gave refuge to and I want to thank you.

Shakur   You can't prove Altaaf is your boy.

Manohar Lal   It has been proven. The authorities have traced him and assured me that he has been living here as your adopted son.

Shakur   He was alone. We looked and waited but no one came to claim him.

Manohar Lal   How could we come during the troubles?

Shakur   Seven years we have looked after him as our own.

Manohar Lal   I'm grateful, but for those seven years I have been searching. Searching everywhere.

Shakur   You don't have to be grateful. It is good you have found us. Now you can go back and be happy. You can tell your wife Altaaf is in a secure home.

Manohar Lal   Bhai, we want our son. If your son was lost, would you not want him back?

Shakur   He is emotionally attatched to us. He's our son.

Manohar Lal   He is mine, my wife bore him. The blood that runs in his veins is mine. When his body turns to ashes, he will be flesh of my flesh.

Shakur   The azan has been read in his ear. He goes to the mosque every Friday. He says his prayers five times a day.

Manohar Lal   I don't care if he has converted.

Shakur   Why uproot him now?

Manohar Lal   I'm not uprooting him. I'm taking him back to his roots.

Shakur   What makes you think he will go with you?

Manohar Lal   Ask him. Let me see him and ask him.

Shakur   You walked past him in the street.

Manohar Lal   Bhai sahib, you are a father. I accept that you have been his father, but he is still my boy.

Shakur   Spare yourself, bhai sahib. He will not even recognise you.

Manohar Lal   I will take my chance.

Shakur   Altaaf, beta. *Idhar aana.*

Pali *comes out, with* **Zainab** *in purdah.*

Shakur   *Beta salaam karo.*

Pali   *A salaam walaikum*

Manohar Lal   *Walaikum salaam.*

(*Internal voice.*)
   He is my Pali –
   I know
   That scar on his chin
   When I pushed him high
   On the swing
   And he fell off.

Shakur   Beta, do you recognise this man?

Pali   Yes.

Shakur *is scared.* **Manohar Lal** *can't believe his luck.*

Pali   He asked us the way. You said he's from India.

Shakur   You see.

Manohar Lal (*taking out a photo*)   May I show him this?

Shakur *nods.*

Manohar Lal   Beta, do you remember the Baisakhi fair? This is my boy. This is my wife carrying baby Gudiya. This is me. Beta, do you remember your mother?

Pali (*in recognition*)   Pitaji, Mataji, Gudiya.

Manohar Lal   Pali. My Pali.

Shakur   Beta. This is your real father. He has come for you. Do you want to go to India with him?

Pali   I want to stay with my ammi and abu.

Shakur   You heard the boy.

Manohar Lal   The law is on my side.

Shakur   We can drag the case on for ever.

Manohar Lal (*pleading to* **Zainab**)   Sister, I am not begging you for my child, I'm begging you for my wife's life. She is like the living dead. The boy's absence has driven her insane. I cannot go back, having found him but empty-handed. Day and night she thinks of him. We have lost our baby girl.

Pali   Gudiya! What happened to our baby?

Manohar Lal   You remember Gudiya? Beta, she is beloved to God.

Pali   She's dead?

Manohar Lal   God had more need of her and called her. You are a mother, sister. Please take pity on my wife. She is like a bird whose nest has been destroyed.

Zainab (*affected by* **Manohar Lal***'s plea*)   Take him. He is yours. Take him. I don't want to hurt an unfortunate woman.

Shakur   What are you saying, Zainab?

Zainab   If the child was ours and we had lost him, think how you would feel. It's a sin to keep a child from his own parents.

Manohar Lal   Sister, I will forever be in your debt.

Zainab   In my heart I have always known he was another's wealth on loan to me. Each year that passed I would pray that the debt be written off and not be recalled.

Pause.

I will part with him on one condition. You must send him to us every year on the occasion of Idd to stay with us for a month.

Manohar Lal   He is your wealth, bahen. You have my word.

Zainab   Come for him tomorrow. He will be ready.

Manohar Lal *leaves.*

Zainab   *Mere soné,* come here.

Pali *doesn't budge, clearly upset.*

Pali   You sendin' me away 'cos I'm bad.

Shakur   No, beta. Who says you're bad?

Pali   I said you wasn't my family and now you don't want me to be your family.

Zainab   You are our whole world.

Pali   Please don't let him take me.

Shakur   He is your pitaji, beta. The roots and tree from where you came.

Zainab   We were lucky to make you ours for a short time.

Pali   Please Ammi, don't send me.

Zainab   Your mataji is bereft without you and your sister. For seven years while you lit up our life, her life has been in darkness.

Pali *starts crying.*

Zainab   Cry. Let the ocean out.

Pali   I won't go. You can't make me. I'm not going.

He runs off.

Scene Six

A little while later. **Buttameez***'s hideout – a barn or makeshift shelter.*

Buttameez   They'll be looking for you.

Pali   I hate them. They want to send me away.

Buttameez   To your real family.

Pali   Who lost me. What makes them think they can get me back?

Buttameez   At least you can get them back. You lucky.

Pali   Don't feel lucky. Is this where you sleep?

Buttameez   Yeah.

Pali   Cool!

Buttameez   Cold, you mean. Freezing in the winter.

Pali   Can I stay here for ever? No one tells you what to do.

Buttameez *shrugs his shoulders.*

Pali   What happened to your family? You never said.

Buttameez   I never told no one. Only the horses.

Pali   Horses? What horses?

Buttameez   The tonga-wallahs let me groom their horses for two annas. They give me food and let me stay here.

Pali   You can't speak to horses.

Buttameez   I can. You have to whisper to them and they answer you back. I trust them and they trust me.

Pali   You can trust me.

Buttameez *(relaxes)*   You really wanna know?

Pali   You know everything about me..

Buttameez *(hesitant as he tells his story)*   All right then . . . First when the bullets started flying over our heads, it was pure

fireworks . . . We'd play dodge-ball but it was like real bullets . . .
People said the white goras had drawn a line on the map and
now the Muslims had to go to a new country . . . Pakistan. I
didn't wanna go, but there was no choice . . . Before we could
leave, the Hindu mob came . . . I recognised our neighbour
and Guddu's dad . . . Guddu was like my best friend, you
know . . . We traded bante and swam in the river . . . My dad
was brave . . . he could, like, actually mash someone if they
even said something about his family . . . He just stood there . . .
I saw them cut off his head and set fire to the house . . . I
climbed to the roof and jumped into a pile of sugarcane chaff.
They didn't see me . . . My legs. I didn't feel the pain. I just hid
there, covered in sugarcane skins and licking them 'cos I was
thirsty . . . and watched my family burn inside . . . They were
screamin' and that . . . At night, I started walking straight . . .
could hardly walk . . . kept asking people . . . 'Where is Pakistan?
Which way?' I crossed the border but I never saw no line.

Pali Can I stay here and be your family?

Buttameez No. I'm no one's family.

Pali Why didn't you get adopted?

Buttameez This old woman wanted me. She said her house
was my house. I said I got no family, I don't need a house. And
a schoolteacher said I could be his son but I didn't want to.
I'm bad luck.

Pali It's not true. I always win if you on my team.

Buttameez Don't want to love anyone else. If you love
people you lose them.

Pali Or they lose you.

Buttameez (*givong his quilt back to* **Pali**) I dried this for you.

Pali Thanks.

He sniffs it.

Smells different. Of river water.

Scene Seven

The next day. The Maidan.

Aisha *and* **Pali** *are hanging around the Maidan, messing around with their marbles or whatever. During this goodbye scene the other children enter.*

Aisha   Just think, you'll get two lots of presents on your birthday. You'll celebrate Diwali and Idd . . .

Pali   Easier to have one mum and dad.

Aisha   Never even seen my dad.

Pali   Who is he? You never said.

Aisha   You never asked.

Pali   So you gonna tell me? Last chance.

Aisha   It's my ammi's secret. I'm a 'love-child'. Special, she says, but I'd rather have a dad.

Pali   You can have one of mine.

Aisha   You might like your real mum and dad.

Pali   I just want everything to stay the same. Friends. Family.

Aisha   My ammi says nothing stays the same. Only her feelings.

Buttameez *and* **Pagal Head** *arrive with* **Hasina**. **Pagal Head** *gives him an old box of marbles.*

Pali   My treasure of bante! From the hidey-hole.

Pagal Head   You can use them to mash up dem Hindu vegetarians. They got no chance.

Buttameez   Remember when we made you eat chicken kebab and pretended it was paneer?

Pali   You tricked me.

Buttameez   But you pure love chicken now.

Pagal Head   You gonna get murghi in India?

Pali   Dunno.

Buttameez   Can't go back to being veggie. Muslims are strong.

Pali   And Hindus are clever.

Pagal Head   But they darpok, innit? Cowards.

Pali   People are people.

Pagal Head *suddenly realises what he's said.*

Pagal Head   You come back on Idd and we suck the bones from the biryani.

The kids say goodbye, and **Pali** *is left with* **Hasina**.

Hasina   Everyone was looking for you yesterday.

Pali   I ran away.

Hasina   But you came back.

Pali   Yeah. When are you going?

Hasina   Today. Same as you.

Pali   You takin' your shoes?

Hasina   No. They've fallen apart.

Pali   Give me a letter for your ammi. I'll deliver it to her when I'm in Delhi.

Hasina   No need.

Pali   I'll be in the same town. Don't you want me to find her?

Hasina   The soft lady wrote to her. She sent her permission for me to be adopted.

Pali   She know where you were?

Hasina   All this time. Said she can't take me back, that I belong here.

Pali   Wonder where I belong?

Hasina   People should belong to each other, not to places.

Pali   I'm sorry.

Hasina   Me too.

Pali   I'll think about you really really hard and maybe you'll think about me at the same time.

Hasina   Maybe.

Pali   You're the one who said.

Hasina   Maybe I was wrong.

Pali   I'll see you when I come back on Idd?

Hasina   Yeah.

Scene Eight

Manohar Lal *and* **Pali** *are in the back of the car travelling back to India.*

Manohar Lal (*internal voice*)
  His body warm
  Against mine
  Thaws the chill
  In my heart.
  I want to shower him
  With my affection,
  But all I can do
  Is steal a glance,
  Looking for signs
  Of connection.
  What's me in him,
  What's him in me?
  He moved on,
  But for me
  Time stood still.

Pali (*internal voice*)
  I prayed and wished
  For him to come,
  But when he came
  I wished my wish
  Hadn't come true.
  He's looking at me
  But I can't look at him.
  I know he's my father
  But he's not my abu.

His rumi cap flies off.

Pali   My cap!

Manohar Lal   Rukko! Stop the car.

He gets out, picks up the cap and puts it back on **Pali**'s *head.*

Manohar Lal   Here, beta.

Pali *looks at* **Manohar Lal**'s *face.*

Scene Nine

Back in India.

Manohar Lal *and their friends are celebrating the return of their son with the singing of a Punjabi festive song.* **Kaushalya** *is resplendent in a red chunri,* **Pali** *is withdrawn. As the song finishes, a* **Man** *and a* **Woman** *congratulate* **Manohar Lal** *and* **Kaushalya** *on* **Pali**'s *return.*

Woman   Who knows the ways of God? The child you held safely to your bosom was snatched by death and the child who strayed away has come back safe and sound.

Man   He's a lucky boy indeed to have had God's protection.

Woman   He's very quiet.

Kaushalya   So much has happened for him.

Pali *quietly gets his prayer mat, lays it down, and starts to do his namaaz, much to the horror of the guests.*

Woman   What's going on, Kaushalya? What is your son doing?

Manohar Lal   He instinctively knows when it's time for namaaz.

Man   Why don't you stop him?

Kaushalya   He's been through so much. He'll learn soon enough.

Man   Manohar bhai, we don't want a Muslim amongst us.

Manohar Lal   They were very good parents to him. They don't have a child of their own. It was natural for them to bring him up as a Muslim. What else could they do?

Man   You know what these people are like. They go round converting because it gets them to Heaven. They've taken one of ours. We can't allow this.

Woman   Next he'll be asking for meat – will you give it to him?

Manohar Lal   Even his tastes will have to change slowly.

Woman   Hai Ram! Have you thought, who will give him their girl if word gets out about all this?

Kaushalya   I can't worry about his marriage just yet. I still have to win his heart.

*The **Man** goes up to **Pali**.*

Man   What were you doing?

Pali   I was saying my namaaz.

Man   We won't allow you to do this thing here. From today, no namaaz, you understand?

Kaushalya   He's only a child, leave him.

Man   Manohar Lal, better call a pandit and a barber. We need to shave his head and make him pure again. Undo this conversion.

Manohar Lal   All in good time, bhai, let him adjust to his circumstances.

Man   You will regret it if you wait a minute longer.

Manohar Lal   There's too much emphasis placed on these things.

Man   You don't care that your son has come back as a Muslim?

Manohar Lal   It is enough for me that my son has come back.

Man   I can't believe my ears. What is your name, boy?

Pali   Altaaf.

Man   No, your name is Pali. Who told you your name is Altaaf?

Pali   My abbaji.

Man   Abbaji. This is your pitaji. Repeat your name five times – Pali, Pali . . . Pali.

Manohar Lal   Please. I will not let you frighten my boy.

Man   Either sort him out or send him back to those Muslims. We won't tolerate this here. (*To* **Woman**.) Chalo.

Woman   Might have been better if he had never been found.

The **Man** *and* **Woman** *leave.*

Manohar Lal (*internal voice*)
 I live among them
 But these are not my people,
 My people
 Cared not for Bhagwan or Allah.
 They shared

Love and lassi
In each other's homes.
What happened, then,
To cause this narrowing of minds
And the broadening
Of this divide?

Pali   I was only doing my prayers.

Kaushalya   I know, but we pray in a different way. We'll
teach you to pray our way and we'll call you Pali again.

Pali   But that's not my name.

He starts crying.

Manohar Lal   Even our hearts are left across the border,
beta. This place will never be home.

Kaushalya   We have had to start again and try to belong.

Pali   People should belong to each other and not to places.

Manohar Lal   Yes, you are right, and we are family.

Kaushalya   When Gudiya was born and you were jealous,
you remember you would run to me and lie on my stomach?
I would wrap my dupatta over you and you would pretend that
you were a baby growing inside me. You came from me, beta,
and now you've come back to me.

Pali *goes into her arms. The beginning of reconnection.*

Scene Ten

Back in Pakistan. **Shakur** *and* **Zainab***'s home.*

Zainab   He's gone and with him has gone all the gaiety of
this house. This time of night I would be searching the streets
for him. He would hide and try to snatch more time with his
friends. I would never know where to find him.

Shakur   Now even his friends have dispersed.

Zainab What do you think? Will he come to visit us on Idd? Will those people send him?

Shakur He looked like a man of his word.

Zainab Yes. Inshallah, we will see him again.

She starts to cry.

Shakur Cry. Let the ocean out.

We end on a soundtrack of children singing 'Lab pe aati he', a prayer of hope by the poet Iqbal.

Methuen Modern Plays

include work by

Edward Albee
Jean Anouilh
John Arden
Margaretta D'Arcy
Peter Barnes
Sebastian Barry
Brendan Behan
Dermot Bolger
Edward Bond
Bertolt Brecht
Howard Brenton
Anthony Burgess
Simon Burke
Jim Cartwright
Caryl Churchill
Noël Coward
Lucinda Coxon
Sarah Daniels
Nick Darke
Nick Dear
Shelagh Delaney
David Edgar
David Eldridge
Dario Fo
Michael Frayn
John Godber
Paul Godfrey
David Greig
John Guare
Peter Handke
David Harrower
Jonathan Harvey
Iain Heggie
Declan Hughes
Terry Johnson
Sarah Kane
Charlotte Keatley
Barrie Keeffe
Howard Korder

Robert Lepage
Doug Lucie
Martin McDonagh
John McGrath
Terrence McNally
David Mamet
Patrick Marber
Arthur Miller
Mtwa, Ngema & Simon
Tom Murphy
Phyllis Nagy
Peter Nichols
Sean O'Brien
Joseph O'Connor
Joe Orton
Louise Page
Joe Penhall
Luigi Pirandello
Stephen Poliakoff
Franca Rame
Mark Ravenhill
Philip Ridley
Reginald Rose
Willy Russell
Jean-Paul Sartre
Sam Shepard
Wole Soyinka
Shelagh Stephenson
Peter Straughan
C. P. Taylor
Theatre de Complicite
Theatre Workshop
Sue Townsend
Judy Upton
Timberlake Wertenbaker
Roy Williams
Snoo Wilson
Victoria Wood

Methuen Film titles include

The Wings of the Dove
Hossein Armini

Mrs Brown
Jeremy Brock

Persuasion
Nick Dear after Jane Austen

The Gambler
Nick Dear after Dostoyevski

Beautiful Thing
Jonathan Harven

Little Voice
Mark Herman

The Long Good Friday
Barrie Keeffe

State and Main
David Mamet

The Crucible
Arthur Miller

The English Patient
Anthony Minghella

The Talented Mr Ripley
Anthony Minghella

Twelfth Night
Trevor Nunn after Shakespeare

The Krays
Philip Ridley

The Reflecting Skin & The Passion of Darkly Noon
Philip Ridley

Trojan Eddie
Billy Roche

Sling Blade
Billy Bob Thornton

The Acid House
Irvine Welsh

Methuen Contemporary Dramatists
include

John Arden (two volumes)
Arden & D'Arcy
Peter Barnes (three volumes)
Sebastian Barry
Dermot Bolger
Edward Bond (seven volumes)
Howard Brenton
  (two volumes)
Richard Cameron
Jim Cartwright
Caryl Churchill (two volumes)
Sarah Daniels (two volumes)
Nick Darke
David Edgar (three volumes)
Ben Elton
Dario Fo (two volumes)
Michael Frayn (three volumes)
David Greig
John Godber (two volumes)
Paul Godfrey
John Guare
Lee Hall (two volumes)
Peter Handke
Jonathan Harvey
  (two volumes)
Declan Hughes
Terry Johnson (two volumes)
Sarah Kane
Barrie Keefe
Bernard-Marie Koltès
  (two volumes)
David Lan
Bryony Lavery
Deborah Levy
Doug Lucie

David Mamet (four volumes)
Martin McDonagh
Duncan McLean
Anthony Minghella
  (two volumes)
Tom Murphy (four volumes)
Phyllis Nagy
Anthony Neilsen
Philip Osment
Louise Page
Stewart Parker (two volumes)
Joe Penhall
Stephen Poliakoff
  (three volumes)
David Rabe
Mark Ravenhill
Christina Reid
Philip Ridley
Willy Russell
Eric-Emmanuel Schmitt
Ntozake Shange
Sam Shepard (two volumes)
Shelagh Stephenson
Wole Soyinka (two volumes)
David Storey (three volumes)
Sue Townsend
Judy Upton
Michel Vinaver
  (two volumes)
Arnold Wesker (two volumes)
Michael Wilcox
Roy Williams
Snoo Wilson (two volumes)
David Wood (two volumes)
Victoria Wood

Printed in the United Kingdom
by Lightning Source UK Ltd.
131296UK00001B/87/A